North Korea

TARA WALTERS

Children's Press®
An Imprint of Scholastic Inc.
New York Toronto London Auckland Sydney
Mexico City New Delhi Hong Kong
Danbury, Connecticut

Content Consultant

Michael Robinson
Professor, Department of East Asian Languages and Cultures
Indiana University
Bloomington, Indiana

Library of Congress Cataloging-in-Publication Data

Walters, Tara, 1973-
  North Korea / by Tara Walters.
        p. cm. -- (A true book)
  Includes index.
      ISBN-13: 978-0-531-16854-7 (lib. bdg.)
                978-0-531-20728-4 (pbk.)
      ISBN-10: 0-531-16854-9 (lib. bdg.)
                0-531-20728-5 (pbk.)

  1. Korea (North)--Juvenile literature. I. Title. II. Series.

DS932.W35 2008
951.93--dc22   2007036226

Produced by Weldon Owen Education Inc.

Find the Truth!

Everything you are about to read is true *except* for one of the sentences on this page.

Which one is **TRUE**?

T or F   There is a lot of traffic in North Korean cities.

T or F   North Korea is involved in the animated movie industry.

Find the answers in this book.

Contents

THE BIG TRUTH!

Cast of Thousands

Portraits of the "Great Leader" are displayed in all public places.

4 From Architecture to Animation

What kind of popular movies are made in North Korea?

5 People and Party

Why do so many children wear a red scarf?

6 City and Village

Is the workers' paradise a shoppers' paradise?

Dancers holding red fans perform in Kim Il-sung (kim ill-suhng) Square. The square is in Pyongyang, the capital.

CHAPTER 1

Closed Society

Kim Il-sung Square is larger than Red Square in Moscow.

People outside of North Korea know very little about life there. Few tourists are allowed to visit. Even fewer North Koreans may leave it. The government controls many aspects of people's lives. Many of North Korea's 23 million people are proud of their government. North Korea is one of the last **Communist** countries in the world.

North Korea and South Korea were once a single country. South Korea is now very modern. It has a booming **economy**. North Korea has fallen behind. Today, it has many economic problems. It has difficulty getting enough electricity. Some people must use candles at home. They plow their fields with oxen. Few people own cars, TVs, or computers.

In recent years, the North Korean government has begun to allow some tourists to visit. These visits are tightly controlled. A guide takes tourists to an approved list of sites. It's nearly impossible for visitors to speak to North Korean citizens.

Posters like these are found all over the country. They heroize the leadership and workers of the country.

Jangbaek Falls is one of several waterfalls on Mount Paektu. Mount Paektu is on the border of North Korea and China.

CHAPTER 2

Hidden Land

Mount Paektu is the highest mountain in North Korea.

North Korea occupies the upper half of the Korean **Peninsula**. South Korea takes up the lower half. North Korea is bordered on the north by China and Russia. The center of the country is mountainous. Plains are found in the west and on the east coast. As in the northern United States, winters are long and cold. Summers are warm and humid.

Heaven Lake

Mount Paektu is a popular tourist destination for Koreans and Chinese. At the top, there is a beautiful crater lake. It is called Heaven Lake. The mountain is sacred to Koreans. Legend has it that it is the birthplace of Korean **civilization**. North Korea's current leader is Kim Jong-il. He claims that he was born on Mount Paektu. His birthplace is a national monument.

The first bicycle factory in North Korea opened in Pyongyang in 2005. It is a joint project with China.

Factories and Farms

North Korea's economy is controlled by the government. The government owns all of the factories and land. The government chooses which crops are grown. It decides which goods are made. It even determines which jobs people may have. Some people are farmers. However, most North Koreans work in factories.

Self-Reliance

The economy of North Korea is strongly influenced by a **philosophy** called juche (JOO-cheh). *Juche* means self-reliance, or autonomy. North Korea's first leader, Kim Il-sung, believed that the country should be able to produce everything that it needs. This includes all food, goods, and services. Unfortunately, juche has not always worked. In the mid-1990s, floods and drought led to terrible **famines**. Many people died or lost their homes. Today, North Korea is a poor country.

However, recent changes are helping to boost the suffering economy. A special industrial zone has been opened in Kaesong (kay-song). This city is near the border with South Korea. More than 12,000 North Koreans now work in factories there. The factories are owned and run by South Koreans.

There are now more than
23 South Korean factories
in Kaesong Industrial Park.

The Pohyon Temple complex
was once a major religious center.
It was founded in 1042 A.D.

大

CHAPTER 3

Divided Kingdom

Thousands of years ago, three kingdoms ruled the Korean Peninsula. They were Koguryo, Silla, and Paekche (behk-cheh). By 668 A.D., the kingdom of Silla had taken over the entire peninsula. Silla was a wealthy kingdom. Its rulers made **Buddhism** the kingdom's religion. Silla rule lasted for more than 200 years.

The temple complex was almost completely destroyed in the Korean War. This temple has been rebuilt.

This vase is a relic of the Koryo kingdom.

In 936 A.D., the Koryo kingdom seized power. Korea is named for this kingdom. The Koryo rulers held power for more than 400 years. During their rule, Korean arts flourished. However, the country had to defend itself continually from invaders. The last traditional kingdom, Choson, lasted from 1392 to 1910. By 1910, Japan had taken control of Korea.

Japan lost control of Korea in 1945, at the end of World War II. The winning nations divided Korea into two parts. In 1948, South Korea became a **republic**, like the United States. North Korea became a Communist country, like the **Soviet Union**.

Kings' Tombs

The Koguryo Tombs are among North Korea's most valued historic sites. Some of them are located around Pyongyang. Others are near the border with China. The murals inside the tombs are very well known. They show scenes of daily life more than a thousand years ago. The statues shown here guard the tomb of King Tongmyong. He was the first Koguryo king.

A New Order

Kim Il-sung was the natural choice to lead North Korea. In 1920, he and his family escaped Japanese rule. They moved to China. There Kim Il-sung learned about Communism. He worked to end Japan's control over his country. During World War II, Kim Il-sung led Korean troops. They joined the Soviet Union against Japan. In 1948, Kim Il-sung became leader of North Korea. He founded the Korean Workers' Party (KWP). This still rules. He also set up a **socialist** system, like that of the Soviet Union.

Time Line of Hope

1972
The first Red Cross conference of North Korea and South Korea is held.

1991
North Korea and South Korea both join the United Nations. This organization works for world peace.

Under this socialist system, Kim Il-sung established a command economy. In a command economy, the government owns all factories. It decides what goods are made. It also decides how much money people will earn. All of the country's land is organized into large farms. People from rural areas work together on these farms. Kim Il-sung led North Korea until he died in 1994. His son, Kim Jong-il, then took over. Kim Jong-il still rules today.

North Korea

South Korea

2000
The first meeting between North Korea and South Korea is held.

2004
Olympic teams from North Korea and South Korea march together under one flag.

21

The War That Has Never Ended

The division of Korea has overshadowed life there since 1948. In 1950, Kim Il-sung invaded South Korea. The Korean War lasted for three years. United States troops supported the South Korean army. The Chinese government supported North Korea. When the war was over, Korea remained divided. A **demilitarized** zone (DMZ) was set up between the two countries. Today, the DMZ is the most heavily guarded border in the world.

The conflict has never been resolved. South Korea never signed the peace treaty. Both Koreas would like to be one country. But each would like its own government to be in charge. Koreans still do not travel freely between North Korea and South Korea.

In May 2007, trains crossed the border between North Korea and South Korea. It was the first time that had happened since the end of the Korean War. The event was celebrated on both sides of the border.

7435

ㄱ간 열차시험운행

7. 5. 17

Cast of Thousands

THE **BIG** TRUTH!

The Arirang Festival is a huge celebration. It was held in 2002, 2005, and 2007. It is famous for its massive human mosaics. These make up the backdrop for the stage. More than 20,000 schoolchildren create the mosaics. They flip colored flashcards in perfect precision. Tens of thousands of gymnasts and dancers also perform. This extravaganza is the biggest of its kind in the world.

Timing Is Everything

Mosaic backdrops show battle scenes. They also show the flag and portraits of Kim Il-sung. The children flip their cards once every 30–60 seconds for a 90-minute performance. Sometimes the pictures almost appear to be animated.

All Together Now

Arirang lasts for two months. Shows take place six days a week. They include acrobatics, military displays, and fireworks. For an entire year, 100,000 people train for their parts. Arirang takes place in the May Day Stadium in Pyongyang. The stadium holds 150,000 people. It is one of the largest stadiums in the world.

25

In this wall painting, President Kim Il-sung guides his son, Kim Jong-il, on the path of leadership.

CHAPTER 4

From Architecture to Animation

Most modern art in North Korea shows one or both of the two Great Leaders.

North Korea shares thousands of years of traditional arts and music with South Korea. However, in North Korea today, the government controls all art. Art is often used to honor the two leaders, Kim Il-sung and Kim Jong-il. Both leaders are credited with creating their own works of art. These include plays, books, and operas.

The Grand People's Study House was built in 1982. Yet its architecture reflects traditional Korean building styles.

Modern Architecture

There are huge monuments to Kim Il-sung, such as the Tower of the Juche Idea. They can be found all over the country. There are many impressive buildings as well. Much of Pyongyang was destroyed in the Korean War. It has since been almost completely rebuilt. Some buildings look ultramodern. Others are built in traditional Korean style.

The Tower of the Juche Idea is 558 feet (170 meters) tall. It was built to celebrate Kim Il-sung's seventieth birthday.

The tower is covered with 25,550 pieces of stone. That is one for each day of Kim Il-sung's life.

Posters and paintings often show happy workers and children. They are meant to show the success of the socialist system.

Art of the State

In North Korea, a special government department is in charge of **propaganda**. Propaganda is considered a form of art. Special art squads travel around the country. They give poetry readings. They perform plays and songs. These performances are intended to inspire the country's workers.

Hidden Talents

Since the 1990s, North Korea has been involved in a high-tech industry—computer animation. North Koreans are respected for their technical skills in this field. They use the latest animation software. They developed the skills and technology they need while making movies for the government. Then they began to work on movie projects from South Korea. Now they do animation work for other countries.

Most of the animation for the movie *Empress Chung* was done in North Korea. The story is based on a Korean folktale. The movie opened in North Korea and South Korea at the same time.

Newlyweds swear loyalty to both
Kim Il-sung and Kim Jong-il.
They place a gift at the feet
of a statue of Kim Il-sung.

CHAPTER 5

People and Party

When North Korea was formed, the government tried to get rid of most traditional culture. Buddhist temples, for example, are now treated as cultural relics. Since 1948, the country's culture has been recreated. It now focuses mainly on admiration of the Great Leader. Kim Il-sung is remembered even at weddings.

Members of the Workers' Party and government must wear a badge of the Great Leader at all times.

Kim Il-sung

Crowds line the streets of Pyongyang. They are watching a military parade.

North Korea's Class System

The government divides North Koreans into three social classes. This affects the jobs and housing each person receives from the government. It even affects the amount of food a person gets. The highest group is the loyal class. It is made up of top people in the KWP, and families of war heroes. To live in Pyongyang, you must belong to this class.

The next group is the ordinary group. People in this group have decent jobs. Food is rationed. But this group usually has enough to eat.

The lowest group is made up of people who are considered disloyal. This may simply be because their relatives sided with the Japanese before World War II. Or it may mean that family members have escaped from North Korea since the Korean War. People in this group are forced to work in mines or on farms.

This is one of 51 farms in a huge goat-farming project.

A Child's Life in North Korea

North Korea puts great emphasis on education. All schooling is free. Today, almost all adults can read and write. As in other socialist countries, political training plays a large role in school. All children must attend school through tenth grade. Only students who get approval from the KWP may go on to higher studies.

Young Pioneers can be spotted by the red scarves they wear.

Many children between nine and fifteen years of age join the Young Pioneers. Children meet for study, sports, and other after-school activities. However, they also study the ideals of juche and socialism. When they are older, they may join the Socialist Working Youth League. This organization works closely with the KWP.

Some subway stations are highly decorated.
They have chandeliers and propaganda murals.
A number of the trains are old trains from East Germany.

CHAPTER 6

City and Village

Slightly more than half of the people of North Korea live in cities. Pyongyang is the country's largest city. It is filled with modern, high-rise apartment buildings. The streets are clean and uncrowded. There are few cars or bicycles. Most people walk or use the excellent subway system. The city also has many large, beautiful parks.

The subway system is deep underground. It doubles as a bomb shelter.

Pyongyang department stores are not usually crowded.

City Life

North Koreans shop mostly in simple stores that sell local products. They buy fruits and vegetables at outdoor markets. To purchase food, people must present food coupons. These are handed out by the government. A few department stores sell items from outside North Korea. Typically, only wealthy people can shop there. A regular worker would need to save for months just to buy a jacket.

Village Life

In a typical North Korean village, houses look alike. Villagers stay close to home, because internal travel is restricted. Youth and KWP groups sometimes travel to the cities to tour the sites and pay their respects to the Great Leader.

Most farms in North Korea are organized into **collectives**. In collectives, workers receive a share of the produce and the money the farm makes. They help manage the collective. State farms are managed by the government. Workers receive wages. Farms often have large apartment complexes for the workers to live in.

위대한 수령 김일성 동지는 우리와 함께 계신다.

Many villages have a large tower. On it, there is a slogan glorifying the state.

41

Winds of Change

North Korea is one of the most closed societies in the world. However, it has taken some first, cautious steps toward change. In 2007, North and South Korea started talking about signing a peace treaty. This would formally end the war of 1950–1953. Many Koreans on both sides of the border now have hope they may one day see their nation united again. ★

This arch was built over a major highway in Pyongyang. It symbolizes a united Korea.

True Statistics

Official name:
Democratic People's Republic of Korea
Size: 46,540 square miles
(120,538 square kilometers)
Major cities: Chongjin, Hamhung, Kaesong,
Nampo, Pyongyang, Sinuiju, Sunchon, Wonsan
Population: Almost 23 million
Life expectancy: 69 years (men),
74 years (women)
Currency: North Korean won (wahn)
Internet country code: kp
Television stations: 4

Did you find the truth?

There is a lot of traffic
in North Korean cities.

North Korea is involved in
the animated movie industry.

Resources

Books

Behnke, Alison. *Kim Jong-il's North Korea* (Dictatorships). Minneapolis: Twenty-First Century Books, 2007.

Gerdes, Louise I. *North & South Korea* (Opposing Viewpoints). Chicago: Greenhaven Press, 2007.

Haberle, Susan E. *North Korea: A Question and Answer Book*. Mankato, MN: Capstone Press, 2005.

Kummer, Patricia. *North Korea* (Enchantment of the World. Second Series). New York: Children's Press, 2008.

Salter, Christopher L. *North Korea* (Modern World Nations). New York: Chelsea House Publications, 2007.

Stein, R. Conrad. *The Korean War Veterans Memorial* (Cornerstones of Freedom). Danbury, CT: Children's Press, 2002.

Walters, Tara. *South Korea* (A True Book™: Geography). New York: Children's Press, 2008.

Organizations and Web Sites

Democratic People's Republic of Korea

www.korea-dpr.com/menu.htm

This is the official Web site for North Korea and the Korea Friendship Association.

Time for Kids

www.timeforkids.com/TFK/teachers/search/1,28225,,00.html?keyword=North +Korea

Read about North Korea in the news.

Places to Visit

Korean War National Museum

303 North 5th Street
Springfield, IL 62705-0299
888-295-7212
www.kwnm.org
Discover the stories of the Korean War veterans and view war artifacts.

The Metropolitan Museum of Art

1000 Fifth Avenue
New York, NY 10028-0198
212-535-7710
www.metmuseum.org/explore/korea/main.html
Visit the museum's first permanent gallery of Korean art.

Important Words

Buddhism (BOO-dizm) – a religion based on the teachings of Buddha

civilization – a highly developed and organized society

collective – a farm that is run as a cooperative, sharing proceeds and management decisions

Communist (KOM-yuh-nist) – referring to an economic and political system in which the government owns all property

demilitarized – not permitted to be used for military purposes

economy – the system in which goods and services are produced, bought, and sold

famine (FAM-uhn) – a great shortage of food

peninsula – a narrow strip of land nearly surrounded by water

philosophy – the beliefs of an individual or group

propaganda – the promotion of ideas to control people's opinions

republic – a type of government in which laws are made by a group of people elected by the country's citizens

socialist – referring to an economic system in which the production of goods is mainly controlled by the government

Soviet Union – a former federation of 15 republics that included Russia and other nations of eastern Europe and northern Asia

Index

About the Author

Tara Walters enjoys traveling to other countries and learning about their history, people, and culture. She loves history and geography so much that she studied it at the University of Notre Dame. She is a first-generation Irish American who spends part of each year in Ireland. Tara lives in New Jersey, with her sons, husband, and two dogs.

PHOTOGRAPHS: Big Stock Photo (Audrey Zyk, United Nations flag, p. 20; Dimitrios Kessaris, Red Cross flag, p. 20); Getty Images (cover; back cover; p. 15; pp. 23–24; p. 29; p. 32; pp. 36–37; p. 41); iStockPhoto.com (p. 28); Martyn Williams (Juche Tower, p.5); © Travel-Images.com (M.Torres, p. 16); ©Shon Ellerton (p. 38; p. 42); Stock.XCHNG (p. 43); TongRo Image Stock (p. 10; p. 12); Tranz: Corbis (p. 6; p. 13; p. 19; p. 26; p. 30; p. 40); Reuters (pp. 8–9; p. 21; p. 31)

The publisher would like to thank Shon Ellerton for the use of his photographs.